Mum

(n) Like Dad only smarter.

URBAN
WORDS

This edition published by Ravette Publishing 2019.

Ravette Publishing Limited
PO Box 876, Horsham, West Sussex RH12 9GH
info@ravettepub.co.uk

ISBN: 978-1-84161-409-0

Printed and bound in India by Replika Press Pvt. Ltd.

The
Boss

(n) Mum.

ЯR
RAVETTE PUBLISHING

Motherhood

(n) An occupation that is not for wimps.

Sacrifice

(n) Going
9 months
without
any wine.

Unconditional

(n) What a Mother's love is. Her temper however is another matter.

Chocolate

(n) The most effective yet the cheapest psychologist on the planet.

Group Project

(n) Time when you relax and watch someone who cares do all the work.

URBAN WORDS

Mother

(n) Someone who is always there for you and also comes into your room without knocking.

Momster

(n) What happens to Mom after she counts to three.

Dust

A grey powdery erial which es a home varm and zzy feeling.

Balanced Diet

(n) A piece of cake in each hand.

Mother

(n) A magical unicorn who can survive on roughly three hours of sleep per night... for months at a time.

Grocery List

(n) What you spend half an hour writing, then forget to take with you to the shop.

Mombie

(n) An exhausted mother who feeds on chocolate and survives on caffeine.

Toddler

(n) Emotionally unstable tiny dictator who can push you to the edge of insanity. Messy and unreasonable.

URBAN WORDS

Sweater

(n) What you put on when your MUM is cold.

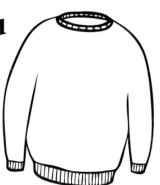

Mother

(n) Woman who gave birth to you and uses that as an excuse to make you do things for her.

Research

(n) What a worried Mum does better than the FBI.

Reality

(n) The annoying time between sleep and internet.

Winter

(n) The three month break between a woman and her razor.

Mother

(n) One person who does the work of twenty, for free.
See also:
Superwoman, Saint

Buttons

(n) Like mums - they hold things together.

Healthy yet delicious
(phr) See "impossible"

Instaglam

(n) Instantly camera-ready thanks to the aid of a fabulous x-pro filter.

Mother

(n) A person with the ability to detect a lie, hear the smallest noises, and see out of the back of her head.

URBAN WORDS

Office

(n) A place to relax after a strenuous night at home.

Beautiful

(adj) Someone whose smile radiates warmth, laughs often and has a heart of gold.

Not bad

(phr) You did way better than I expected, but I'm too proud to admit it.

Mum

(n) The most wonderful person in the world who will love you forever.

URBAN WORDS

Novinophobia

(n) Fear of running out of wine.

URBAN
WORDS

And relax...

(phr) Said no
Mum ever.